Conrad Swiatek

The Piccadilly Tales

With apologies to Geoffrey Chaucer

2:

ISBN: 978-1-291-97673-1

To Rosemary – for putting up with my whims

4:

Contents

General Prologue

Here beginneth the book of the Piccadilly Tales

It's April with its bloody frequent showers,
Big Issue seller in a mud-streaked doorway cowers,
And past him stream the wage-bond masses
Inhaling lead-free traffic gases.
Oh bugger Canterbury, we praise Mammon,
We need to bring home wine and salmon,
And so to grubby platform edge we stream
To get to work; work; one day live the dream…
Our Piccadilly pilgrimage perchance?
We normally make no song and dance,
Ignore the others, sociopaths?
Too many Londoners – do the maths!
Till one day – suddenly – power lost,
Train in mid-tunnel stops. No longer tossed,
The passengers, silent, wait to move again…
A minute passes – two – five – ten…
Driver sick? A power-cut, or bomb?

No info through the intercom.

Now, reader, please suspend your disbelief;

I know commuting folk would now as lief

Blow out their brains as pass the time

Exchanging tales in prose or rhyme,

But let's suppose to pass the hours

Their latent narrative-potential flowers –

'Tis said in each of us a book resides

(Which notion every publisher derides) –

But would the issues in the tales we tell this day

Differ much from those that Chaucer did survey?

Well, as it happens, I was in that carriage trapped

And curious eyes on fellow travellers clapped –

Whilst wondering what their trials and pleasures,

They suddenly all shared their treasures

And none of them their counsel kept

…though 'tis more likely that I slept.

Now each in turn will take the stage

And I'll shut up – so turn the page!

The Whistle-Blower's Tale

The first commuter who to the others spoke

Said he was a decent sort of bloke;

A computer programmer was he,

A Secret Service employee.

Equations linear and quadratic knew he well

And algorithms programmed which would smell

Out treason like the Witchfinder General

Catching web-borne traffic, though ephemeral.

He'd toyed with microphones directional,

And drones and electronics quite exceptional.

He'd been recruited through a competition,

Entered through his own volition,

In a paper which had advertised

No job but just a fifty dollar prize.

He said, "I'll tell you, as it's in this morning's papers,

That the Government is up to sneaky capers:

Whilst we the fiction assiduously renew

That the internet's secure for me and you,

We'll find the messages that count

(Though *you* can't hold us to account)."

What departmental heads alas knew not

Was that, said he, they'd also jot

Down comments damaging and dangerous,

Cantankerous or merely frivolous

From Opposition activists and Reds

Who could no longer hide beneath our beds…

But wait, the leak came not from our city,

This traveller was just a Walter Mitty.

And powers so draconian

Weren't used since times Wilsonian.

…Or were they?

(Afterthought – "Why did they recruit me? Perhaps they advertised in the wrong paper?")

The Policeman's Tale

The tale of leaking matters to the press

Did not a doughty constable impress

Who likewise sat within that carriage.

He, not entirely happy in his marriage,

Then told a tale of private woe,

Which also to the press did go

(Though not by agency of his)

Pertaining to a somewhat brazen Ms.

"I'm not one quick to titillate

When faced with porn – I'm quite irate,

'No trousers' day on London's Tube

Is crime to me, not just a boob,"

Said he. And here the author must make clear

For authenticity sincere

(To Chaucer, with apologies,

Though I feign not his true qualities)

That bawdiness hereafter follows:

If references to her who spits or swallows

Offend the reader, go no farther!

If "queynte" (viz. "cunt") provokes a lather,

Pass on – the next tale is much purer,

Though doubtless told with less bravura.

This officer, upstanding, honest,

Fell quite in love with maid dishonest,

With form for theft, blackmail and fraud,

But with a heavenly body, Lord!

Who, though never known hard drugs to take,

Nor conceal items jail to break,

She ended up in tear-proof suits,

By stripping to her bra and boots.

In interviews our PC's tongue was tied

As he pondered what's inside

And sometimes gained a surreptitious view

And every time his interest grew.

He started meeting her at home,

And there at last his hands did roam.

Then one night when nicked at ASDA

(Before she made it to her Mazda)

Loaded with white goods and cider

This petty criminally-minded spider,

When she arrived late at the nick

And glanced around, all sly and quick,

Was pleased to see who was on duty

And thought, "I'll cash in on my beauty".

Alas, he thought not of his training

Or any shred of pride remaining!

I cannot tell you what then followed

(I've already used a rhyme for swallowed),

But all I'll say is unbeknown

To him, if he did kiss or even roam,

The camera in the cell was running

And caught her plan, though it was cunning,

And the press somehow the sordid tape acquired:

Thus his career soon expired.

And if you think the tale is tall,

It requires but factual changes small*

(The Police I can exonerate,

And maybe I exaggerate)

To illustrate how honey-traps

Can catch those who *should* know they *may not* lapse.

(*I'll own a tabloid was my source,

Where every word was true, of course…

Or are you the kind of person, who, irate,

Says, "Journalists exaggerate –

It can't be true, it must be phony,

That man is never Berlusconi!"

When on the news on Channel 4

He seemed a traffic-warden to "adore"?)

The Management Consultant's Tale

"I am a Jack of all trades and of none –

I'll tell you how your business should be run.

But please do not my brain pollute

With business details too astute,

For I'll impose what's now in vogue

E'en if your staff call me a rogue.

I'll take down all partition walls

And dream up half-baked protocols."

Thus spoke the management consultant while

She half-suppressed a beatific smile.

Her thoughts were not at home just then

Where builders – stout, determined men –

Had greeted her as she was leaving.

Not knowing they were then conceiving

A plan so sweet, nor recognising

Any of those then conniving,

She half-thought that she knew some faces

But couldn't link them to old places…

A trick of memory, to be sure

(No time to ponder thoughts obscure) –

She cast the thought away and counted

Profits as the stairs she mounted.

These builders' boss had once employed her;

Now their frustrated *Schadenfreude*

And revenge exquisitely delightful

Would compensate them for her actions frightful –

They'd been employed to fit a lavvy

(Hardly work that needs a navvy).

"We'll do the work in just one day, ma'am",

Which reassurance made her feel calm.

The room was meant to be positioned

Beneath the stairs and not commissioned

Was any work of demolition,

Rearrangement, transposition.

But as ye sow, so shall ye reap:

When she came home how she did weep,

16:

For changes in the architectural branch

She had imposed, she did not blanch,

Were mirrored in her own abode.

There were no walls twixt her commode,

Her kitchen or the open road!

The Tale of the Lavatory Cleaner

I have a hard-won PhD,

Several languages I speak fluently;

I had to flee from civil war,

Against the odds I landed on this shore.

My neighbours, though, weren't too delighted –

And some have subsequently been indicted

For revealing a violent disposition

After failing to read "…atrician"

After "Paedi…." on a wall plaque

In clear letters, tall and jet-black.

As if a paedo, they surmised,

Had chosen thus to advertise!

These are the folk who, though they're yobs,

Complain I'm stealing all their jobs.

They cannot see my "theft" is venial

And all the jobs that I can get are menial.

The Priest's Tale

I am a Doctor of Divinity,

My Thesis was on Arianism and the Trinity;

I passionately felt the Creed was Gospel truth,

A view I'd had from very tender youth.

I'm privileged as pastor of my flock

To hold the hands of those in shock,

To wed the blissful, name a child,

Encourage morals, bless the mild.

Yet certainty is what I lack.

On God I have not turned my back,

But what "God" is, I cannot say.

Part of me, I'll own, feels no dismay:

Why should it matter if we cannot comprehend

Why succour seems from heaven to descend,

Why light and goodness come from nature or from friend?

All religions cannot be the Truth, it seems…

And yet…

Perhaps they can if, shorn of dogma and extremes,

The spirit, not the letter, is the essence we retain?

I know the Parish would my new-found views disdain,

I ought to tell them, but I vacillate,

I wonder how to broach it, then procrastinate…

Durham's former Bishop did once say

The Gospels chucked in miracles and angels to convey

A sense of wonder, though not literally true.

Yet, though I share this point of view,

I feel I'm called upon to care for those in need, in pain, in joy,

And that *my* Bishop here a different cleric would deploy.

Is it hypocrisy to preach to those whose faith is sturdier than mine?

What matter the vessel if still sweet's the wine?

The Autistic Savant's Tale

I'll tell my tale and hope my bitter pain

May cause a social worker or a teacher to refrain

From thinking that there is but one way to be sane,

Or "normal" – how I loathe that loaded word!

How often, from my comfortable world transferred

To noise, exposure, "interaction" quite absurd-

For what? So that my parent's quest for one like them

Might to fruition come! Me they'd condemn,

And crush like pristine apples in a press:

Self-contained perfection quite immune to stress,

Meditative microcosm. Crushed.

Outward signs of "disability" hushed.

I interact when interaction's due now,

But nine times out of ten you misconstrue, how,

Why, when, to talk: pleasantries, hullabaloo…

From how I look at it the world's askew:

You talk when you have nothing to communicate,

Yet on your every word I'm forced to wait.

If my condition were the norm, not yours,

Your spoken diarrhoea I would pause!

And

enjoy

the Silence.

The Lottery-Winner's Tale

I used to be an honest man
In rented flat, with just one van
(admittedly propped up on bricks),
But happy, living in the sticks.
The two chief joys of my existence
Were booze and betting – otherwise, subsistence.
One-arm-bandits were my forte –
I was so good I could have taught, eh?
I knew which ones would pay out soon –
Spontaneous payment was a boon!
Some claimed if, penniless, I'd tire
Of winning nought, a certain wire
('Twas merely part of my attire,
Got somehow stuck when going through the dryer)
Would find its way into the slot
And thus ensuring that I got
A fair return on money wagered

(for I am equitably natured).

All lies, I say, they'll never prove it:

I always managed to remove it.

E'en so my friends, who knew me better,

Vouched I was an honest better.

When in the boozer (I'd be broke again),

They'd buy the rounds - and I would "words of wisdom" gain:

Betting, they said, was wasteful, frightening,

Lower odds on being struck by lightning,

By meteor smashed to smithereens,

Or hunted down by wolverines –

"The lottery? You'll never win!

Like shoving money in the bin!

And, mate, stop gaming on machines:

You'll never be a man of means!"

Ha!

The last laugh was not theirs but mine!

But how'd I choose my lucky line?

24:

My methods here were far from logical,

My luck was surely astrological:

I'd pick the numbers on a whim,

Let digits in my mind's eye swim,

A birth date here, a dress size there,

Repeat my lucky numbers which would bear

A smaller pay-out oft as not...

Until one day, glued to the spot,

I watched the balls roll on the telly:

38 (circumference of my belly),

42 (year mum was born in),

11 (time to get up in the mornin')

And so on, with tension mounting,

And my luck the odds surmounting,

Until the last dropped into place:

You should've seen my gob-smacked face!

A new phase of my life had started,

Waters hitherto uncharted!

They said they'd help me to invest –

Oh yeah? Get stuffed! Like they knew best!

Stock-market changes rob your money

Insiders only profit – funny!

There's plenty there, will last for ages,

I'll ignore the grasping sages

(Doubtless by commission paid):

I'll splash my money, travel and get laid,

I'll buy the neighbour's house and knock it down

(That bloke is loathed by everyone in town)!

And, sure enough, I trudged my reckless path,

With trophy girlfriends sharing every bath,

My diamond-studded knuckles glimmered starry,

And now propped up on bricks was my Ferrari

(Which my mechanic thought was just obscene, 'e

Didn't know that I preferred my Lamborghini!).

My friends, I found, were always thick as thieves,

Both old and new, but mainly *chez moi* heaves,

Or heaved (it heaves no more) with all the latter –

The nicest – they were always quick to flatter.

26:

I liked my kindness to bestow on them:

A car, or flat – for friendship or, ahem,

For other services received in kind;

I became a connoisseur of altered states of mind!

And once again my old friends were quite wrong

(The old ones, not the new with thong and bong)

When they said I'd made my fortune now for life,

Me, with simple pleasures and no kids or wife.

Surprising just how quickly you can blow

A seven figure sum when you bestow

A yacht, a racehorse, property or car,

From time to time, on family afar

(That's distant both in kinship and in miles),

Especially when keeping up with styles

And fashions.

      Now, again, I'm on the dole,

But if I'm in a black financial hole,

I know my friends from those who loved me only

For my money, so I won't be lonely –

True friends – they comfort me when people say

It's quite outrageous for the state to pay

My upkeep when I squandered all that loot.

If I don't don blue-collar or a suit,

Should I starve? I dished out not just bonhomie,

Alone I saved my town's economy!

The Tale of the Member for Bray

I grew up in a genteel home in Surrey,

New development, by fields doused with slurry,

Two cars in the drive, no duck-house or moat!

My parents' instinct always was to vote

Conservative, and as a girl I'd promote

Their party, taking leaflets out to post

("You'll be fine", said Dad, in Telegraph engrossed)

Through letterboxes on the nearby estate,

Avoiding fractious residents, irate

At Maggies's presidential visage

Dropping onto doormats. Privilege

And selfishness, they assumed, contributed

To my psychology, whilst wealth redistributed

Did not. Though actually the words they threw

Turned the air, ironically, non-Labour blue!

I left suburbia, lacy curtains, potpourri,

Became a student at the LSE.

I realised I'd been moronic

Distributing the bosses' trash, whilst chronic

Unemployment, shoddy urban housing,

Were causes which I should have been espousing.

Arthur Scargill, Len McCluskey, heroes both,

To them, not Thatcher, I would plight my troth!

Students and workers of the world united

Will see capitalist leeches soon indicted!

But let us not dwell on the past too long:

My present constituents would not throng

To any soap box on which I perched

If they knew that to the left I'd lurched

In times gone by when clarity of vision

Was clouded, and beery shouts of derision

In union bars were aimed at those

Whose cause is now the one which I, experienced, chose.

'Trickle-down' no longer means you piss on him

Who labours for a pittance in the dim

And noisy factory; rather, like the breeze,

It animates a forest-full of trees,

It blows a hundred barques across the seas -

Job-creation brings both wealth and ease.

Have I consultancies, directorships?

A lass whose residence between two homes she flips?

And did I get a job with Daddy's firm

Before my new-found views I did affirm?

(And do these questions make me squirm?)

Yes and yes and no and no!

                I'll confirm

The truth and spurn (or sue) the critic who

Suggests I have no real point of view!

Though if I see which way the wind is blowing,

And my voters' euroscepticism growing,

I'll ditch the Tories and to UKIP I'll go skipping -

You kip if you want to, the Lady's not for kipping!

The Entomologist's Tale

In growing up don't lose your inner child;
Select a job which keeps you young and wild.
Invertebrates and exoskeletons galore:
These things I have adored since I was four!
At larval stages soft, pulsating, white –
Then pupa, puss alive, does reunite
A soup of genes: from chaos order flows;
Next myriad forms take flight, display or come to blows
In mediaeval armour with a psychedelic twist.
Even the most "disgusting" would be missed:
Indeed my livelihood depends on those
Which on putrescent body do disclose
The time of death, with testimony mute.
Still others feed on foliage or on fruit –
Drosophila – you love dew and I love you!
OK, reluctantly I do admit it's true
That I'm perceived as somewhat too obsessive,

But I'm still free whilst you've become repressive.

When did you last allow yourself the time

To contemplate the feathery, sublime

Symmetry of moth antennae, or see

The iridescent beetle on a tree –

A prism of joy against the dark, gnarled bark?

The Interpreter's Tale

A couple of linguists called Sapir and Whorf

Thought languages personal experience can morph,

That all that you see 's viewed through *linguistic* specs,

Not tinged just by character, nurture or sex.

A minor example, though interesting too,

Is that Homer said 'wine-coloured' when he meant blue,

For that's what he said when describing the sea

(Unpolluted – not Boston! –by large crates of tea).

And though others have scorned this hypothesis since,

To dump it completely elicits a wince

From people like me, who hope it is true,

Have split personalities, allegiance to two

Cultures and languages –neither and both –

34:

Mid-Atlantic, pan-national – as Heidegger quoth

"Language: the house in which we all dwell" –

Well I have got five, so isn't that swell?!

Though Sophocles also said what God hates most

Is the idiot who brays with a big-headed boast –

And it simply so happens I grew up with two,

So that was a head start, or *Vorsprung*, which you

May not have had – you could say that I cheated!

Now the French got upset because English defeated

All other tongues – even, they say with dismay,

"*Le Traité de Versailles a été écrit en anglais!*"

I'd add, *mes amis*, for what it is worth

Did you know there are more human beings on earth

Who speak two tongues than one (and could add, with rancour,

That neither's a *lingua* which could be called *Franca*!)?

And thus it may be we have less need than most

To learn foreign lingos, but just leave this coast

And, living adventurously, give it a try –

And enjoy new perceptions beneath a green sky!

The Knitter's Tale

Purl two,

    pass one round the back,

        knit four,

Cable four…

    Finger addiction before

Texting, social media; just like whittling wood

Creative, useful – something good,

Individual – or, indulging some sadistic whim,

Unwearable, unflattering, a present for him

(Never liked, not good enough for her).

Occupies the hands, though I'd prefer

If it occupied the mind a little more

Because, though harmless, I have a niggling flaw:

Persistent thoughts of causing someone pain

(be it stranger or myself - am I insane?),

As I wield my needles, creep unbidden.

I shock myself, I keep this dark side hidden,

And worry I am on a path which leads

To dropping cats in bins or throwing seeds from weeds

On pristine lawns, or poking sleeping drunks

Or shearing mohicans from the heads of punks.

And I consider in these moments of black fear

How, when Parisian tumbrils had drawn near,

Disgorged their load and the drums were still,

Before the guillotine's blade fell in the autumn chill,

All that was heard, *mesdames et messieurs*,

Was the clicking of the tricoteuses.

The New Violin Pupil's Parent's Tale

I still haven't got the hang of the fact

That at any time I might be attacked

By auditory train-wreck, hyena impaled,

By screeching of horse-hair on metal assailed,

Believing myself secure in my home,

Whilst washing the dishes or squirting out foam

To clean off some lime-scale or polishing chrome.

It's after three-thirty, I should be aware

That now's not the time to relax in a chair.

I should get out the hoover, escape to the garden,

Maintain that fixed smile and not beg her pardon.

I mustn't discourage, I mustn't belittle,

She could even be England's next Tasmin Little

(If I can't be supportive, at least noncommittal).

With well hidden ear-plugs I hear school recitals

And look in confusion at programmes and titles:

Was that really Mozart? It sounded like Ives

Or Birtwistle played on a blackboard with knives!

But then I remember that I was once learning,

Recall that my parents were likewise once yearning

For rapid improvement, and so on returning

Eschewing the hoover, I smile and beseech:

"Play something for Mummy." "OK Mummy" –
Screeeeech.

The Pedant's Tale

I get irate, I get quite frantic,

My personality is what you'd call pedantic.

I'd make misusing words against the law;

At those who mangle grammar I'd guffaw

And encourage you to follow suit –

Don't leave just yet – just eat and shoot!

Berlin trusted when the wall came down

That language would unite the town –

And though German speakers Swiss and Austrian

Have different words to say "pedestrian",

They try to keep their language pure –

Yet English speakers would such things abjure.

A Lingo Quango's what we lack most -

Yet such a thing the French do boast.

Their own *Academie* stops innovation

Anglo-Saxon imports, word inflation.

I trust you do not disagree?

Neologisms make me turn and flee.

My English is as clear as crystal

(My accent comes from east of Bristol).

Yet what it seems I cannot see

Is the fallacy of etymology –

I'd freeze the meaning of a word today,

But why not change it back to Shakespeare's day?

Or why stop there? Was Chaucer's English "best"?

How far should I delve back in my "pure" quest?

Should proto-Indo-European resurge

Whilst English, Sanskrit, Russian, French submerge?

The Author's Tale

When living in a village do not stoop
To denigrating neighbours, never snoop,
Never gossip! Goldfish bowls are far too small
To provide material for the writer's scrawl,
Which, when published, leads to such a brawl!
(And believe me, it will last, it's no short squall.)
My friends and family did at once divine
Which characters were they and which mine
Alone from purest fantasy. A novel
Needs a theme and people, but you'll grovel
For forgiveness if you want to keep on living
There amongst them! They'll keep sieving
Through and seeing rightly – then embellishing:
Convinced on them the dirt you're dishing.
They'll cross the street and murmur "liar",
You'll be the number one pariah.
You'll yearn for fame – but then regret it!

It's only if the book sells that they'll get it.

My racist mother, homophobic spouse,

Before, as meek and mild as a mouse,

Both roared with fury, they the jury,

And the executioners! Yes, Yuri

Gagarin's Vostok, far from Earth,

Would have been the nearest risk-free berth –

From mine at home I instantly was barred,

No supper cooked – and on the table stood a card

Recalling a supermarket where they sell

Sarnies…

      Though not indulgences to 'keep me out of hell'!

The village lawyer mentioned in my book

An instant loathing to me took –

She is the only lawyer who lives here,

So who I'd based "Liz" on was clear –

And threatened that she'd drag me through the courts:

I wish I'd painted her with fewer warts!

Before you think the day-job's gruesome

And chuck it in, consider twosome

Living, married life, before you choose to walk the plank…

And only do it if the prank

Is worth it!

The Healthy-Eater's Tale

I'm sixty-nine and fit and healthy!

Though Father Time is mean and stealthy,

I won't succumb, for all I eat

Is fat-free, New Age, raw, replete

With antioxidants and berries,

Linseed, primrose, walnut oils and cherries.

I look online and what is best, LOL,

Is I know how! I read cholesterol

In quails' eggs does not appear;

Dandelion roots and wormwood strike no fear

Into my slowly beating, healthy heart.

Of parasites my system now is purged –

New hypothesis – damn hygiene! Now I'm urged

To bring them back, for without flora

My gut is slacking, defences poorer!

Red wine, I'm told, is good, then bad…

I can't keep up – I'm going mad!

46:

I *will* keep up! With *every* fad!
My car is not the latest model,
On designer heels I never waddle,
And though I am no fashionista,
You could call me a fadonista!
I don't care if the flavours clash,
Or if my food is tepid mash,
I'll still be here eschewing treats
And chomping on marsupial meats,
Whilst those friends on a normal diet
Forsake me, for I won't be quiet.
Have a goji berry, dear!

The Unemployed Actor's Tale

Quite why I chose such a cruel, thankless calling –

Where contracts are short-term and critics kept mauling

My efforts – I know not, and so I gave up.

Yet we, inconveniently, still need to sup,

And also, let's face it, my wife misses Prada,

So that's when it struck me that those skills from
RADA

Were useful in interviews, painting illusions,

Assisting employers in reaching conclusions

That I was the keenest of all who applied

For their dead-end job. So, with hair freshly dyed,

I'd go, sporting a goatee, in corduroy jacket,

Then move onto pinstripes when I couldn't hack it

And try to secure one which brought in some more,

Before I was rumbled and kicked out the door.

Then staring in mirrors, endeavouring to re-tie

A crisp Windsor knot, my curriculum vitae

(Fictitious, of course) in my mind I would draft

To send to the latest employer too daft

To spot that the Edinburgh accent I spoke

Was simply a thespian, gargantuan joke.

 And sometimes I managed to put off my sacking

By throwing long sickies – I never was lacking

Ideas (and face paint), so, pale yet courageous,

I coughed and I spluttered. "Looks bad, looks contagious,"

They anxiously muttered, "Don't come in tomorrow,

The rest here can manage – perhaps we can borrow

Maria or Mavis from customer services?

(Though, looking at sickness, the fact is that Mavis is

Almost as poorly as him.)"

But just as the task

Of providing good references so as to mask

Such imperfect abilities started to look

Rather grim, I found old employers would book

Me, because, unbeknown to me, a talent

Which I had was good! For convincing and gallant,

Though ignorant, devious, mendacious and bad

At, say, stacking of shelves, or when needing to add

Ghastly columns of numbers, or making an effort each time

To apply the same rule – if you needed to lime

Like a bird-catcher, grab like a poacher

A client unwilling to buy…

        Well! How to approach her

Persuade and beguile her or even reproach her

Whilst keeping her sweet, always quite on your side,

Was easy as pie for me I will confide;

Now, delighting for ages the staff with my speech

Whilst standing on stages – its blagging I teach.

The Diplomat's Tale

I grew up at a time with a world view quite clear:

There was our bloc and their bloc and, boy, they were near!

With missiles all primed and all facing each other,

Would Cold War turn hot, German brother fight brother?

Yet this, I assumed, would somehow be stable;

With nuclear oblivion neither was able

To alter the other – just broadcasts and spies,

Propaganda and summits, and decrypts and lies.

Then down came the wall and a new threat arose

As, youthful, I through Civil Service ranks rose

In embassy compound with barbed-wire and steel:

The suicide bomber no pity would feel

"Redressing the balance" in his own perception

Between what was holy and Western deception.

I regretted the fact that Bush talked of "Crusades"

(What kind of advice did he get from his aides?),

And when he said states were *with* him or against

The U.S. position, he thus plainly fenced

All neutrals with hostiles, thus causing dismay –

And I don't even mention Guantanamo Bay.

It's in such surroundings my job is so tough!

Whether oil, religion, remark off the cuff

Is your *casus belli*, please learn from the past,

And though it is trite, I'd like to say last

That events, dear boy, tend to go round in circles;

Now Deutschland, united, with Kohl or with Merkel 's

No longer the cauldron, the focus for friction,

We need to be watchful where new threats appear,

Be that in Iraq or in North Korea.

Is the bear still asleep? Will it soon put the boot in?

Is history repeating from Khrushchev to Putin?

And though there are conflicts we cannot avoid,

Dictators where surely troops *must* be deployed,

We must try to see the world view of the other

Before we just lurch from one war to another.

The Sixth-Former's Tale

I'm halfway through AS exams
Considering, midst many Uni spams
(Emails unsolicited and sought),
Which degree is right for me. I ought,
I thought, researching options, puzzled,
As I clicked my mouse and diet Pepsis guzzled,
To speak to those who've qualified and work,
Earn reasonable amounts and drive a Merc,
What satisfaction from their jobs they gain.
What a mistake! Let me explain
What it was that left me quite depressed –
Not a modicum of pleasure was confessed
By doctor, lawyer, teacher or *au pair*;
It isn't what it used to be: despair!
The government has buggered up my job,
The funding's cut, my boss is such a knob...
I wouldn't recommend it to you dear,

Of this and that profession just steer clear.

And yet they haven't tendered resignations,

Their unions still keep up negotiations –

Is it so bad? Or do they relish doom?

Mid-life crisis? Fleeting bust now after boom?

And only one was happily employed

In a job that left me hardly overjoyed:

Cleaning and inspecting midst the stench

Of London's sewers - claimed it was a wrench

To come up blinking into open-air

(With tousled sewage-smelling hair)!

Particularly pleasing, in the main,

Whilst cleaning mounds of fat which blocked the drain,

He marvelled at the engineering feat

Which lay unnoticed underneath our feet.

And yet, in spite of every eager word,

My career won't be thus interred,

Nor based on smoothing passages for turds –

I'll join all the office herds

Or closeted computer nerds…

The Perfumer's Tale

We humans are creatures beneath a veneer –

And fearing our animal nature appear,

Bubbling up from the depths and defacing the varnish,

We put on an act, lest our image it tarnish.

Most people, when questioned, suggested to me

If canine, then sight hounds, not scent hounds, we'd be;

For science and sculpture and reading from books

Are visual, cerebral – the human who looks

For wisdom the species acquired outranks

Any primate unconsciously searching the banks

Of a river or tree top reliant on smell.

That's not an advanced sense! No kingdom yet fell

Through spreading of odours delightful or rank

(Though many a government's policies stank)!

But what do we know of reptilian brains?

We've got one with bolt-ons! Darwinian chains

Still govern deep feelings we don't understand.

But here enter smell, enter pheromone, gland

And neuro-receptor and quantumy things

(Alas I'm not versed in), but what always rings

True is that nothing on earth quite evokes

A fireside chair, hearing grandfather's jokes,

Or grandmother's kitchen when I was just able

By craning my neck to see over her table,

Than smelling plum chutney or wood smoke, you see?

And maybe we pick up subliminally

Arousal of partner or sweat showing fear?

And so we feel anxious, or sexy, or steer

Clear of that ruffian (or try not to leer

At buxom young bar maids while sipping cold beer)

Without higher hominid neural ennui:

For Jekyll and Hyde come together to make

The statesman, the artist, the monk or the rake.

So do not neglect the olfactory sense

And henceforth your pleasures will be more intense.

The Procrastinator's Tale

Doubtless you think that my tale won't be long

But, though I procrastinate, you would be wrong,

Unlike "apathy ru…" sprayed onto a wall,

I finish my task, keep my eye on the ball.

Like stubbornness, mine is a virtue maligned,

A superior art and serene state of mind –

Apart, as you know, when time starts running out,

You rely on another or suffer a bout

Of last minute jitters, or back-ache or flu,

When the plumbing is leaking or essay is due…

I delete first-time emails and only reply

To red-letters and chase-ups, whilst pie-in-the-sky

That's promised by spammers I don't read at all,

Nor donate to good causes from here to Nepal.

And one of these days I might have a child,

But that day can wait, till some money I've piled

For nappies and stretch suits and all that palaver,

I don't see the need now to get in a lather;

Indeed I have heard that the future is happy

For childless couples: no baby, no nappy;

No tantrums nor teething, no cloth when it vomits,

Or visits to doctors for stitches or grommets!

Biological clocks may continue to tick –

 I'll just have one baby before age must flick

The off-switch for parenthood. When will that be?

I'll give it some thought, but I'll first make some tea.

The English Teacher's Questions

Dispirited youngsters, who think they're no good,

Have a marvellous faculty, if see it they could:

Though particle physics may be out of reach,

They all have the powerful tool that is speech.

Man's greatest invention, hard-wired in us all,

Is taken for granted from when we were small.

Tell me, *are* there such things as a feeling or thought

Shorn of the language in which they are caught?

Does consciousness stem from the fact that we think,

Philosophise, argue with words which can link

Your thoughts with my thoughts, with future and past,

And thus make them last?

Destination

Lights briefly dimmed, then engines hummed, aboard

Relief for one and all as, power restored,

The train lurched forward, gently gathered speed

And, from the tyranny of focus freed,

The cable-bundles on the tunnel wall

Gained life, began to rise and fall

With serpentine momentum writhing

In the dark. Then into daydreams scything

Sudden words announcing Piccadilly Circus,

Our next station – so I'd missed mine! Work us

Till we drop, they do: no wonder that I slept.

With hazy head I'm not at all adept

At squeezing through an overcrowded train,

And, as I tried, I stopped and paused. The cause?

A plaintive voice - "You haven't told us yours!"

The characters and stories in this collection are all fictional. Where circumstances from news items in the public domain have sparked a theme, that is all they have done: the characters in this book are not based on any real people. Themes provide platforms for flights of fancy.